THE **FUTURE** OF **POWER**

HARNESSING
WIND
ENERGY

NANCY DICKMANN

NEW YORK

T0027061

Published in 2017 by
The Rosen Publishing Group, Inc.
29 East 21st Street, New York, NY 10010

Cataloging-in-Publication Data
Names: Dickmann, Nancy.
Title: Harnessing wind energy / Nancy Dickmann.
Description: New York : PowerKids Press, 2017. | Series: The future of power | Includes index.
Identifiers: ISBN 9781499432152 (pbk.) | ISBN 9781499432671 (library bound) |
   ISBN 9781508153337 (6 pack)
Subjects: LCSH: Wind power--Juvenile literature. | Wind turbines--Juvenile literature. |
   Renewable energy sources--Juvenile literature.
Classification: LCC TJ820.D54 2017 | DDC 333.9'2--dc23

For Brown Bear Books Ltd:
Editor: Tim Harris
Editorial Director: Lindsey Lowe
Children's Publisher: Anne O'Daly
Design Manager: Keith Davis
Picture Manager: Sophie Mortimer

Picture Credits: t=top, c=center, b=bottom, l=left, r=righ. Interior: 123rf: 28, T.W. Urk 17t, 22, Vaclav Volrab
21b, Tomasz Wyszolmirski 24, Rudmer Zwerver 12; Emaze: 13; MIT: Altaeros Energies 29; NASA: 15; Noedex
Online: 27; Shutterstock: Bildagentur Zoonar GmbH 9, 25, Tilman Ehrcke 17b; Thinkstock: isockphoto 19,
Medioimages/Photodisc 5; Wikipedia:11, ChristianT 21t, Alexi Kostibas 14-15b, W. Schmidt 6, taplondon/
Peter Musgrove 10.

Manufactured in the United States of America
CPSIA Compliance Information: Batch #BW17PK: For Further Information contact Rosen Publishing, New York, New York at 1-800-237-9932

CONTENTS

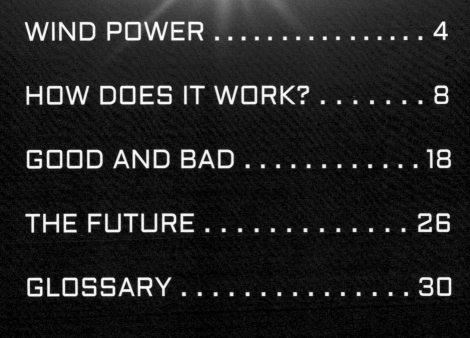

WIND POWER

The natural world is constantly in motion. Winds blow over the land, the ocean swells rise and fall, rivers cascade over waterfalls, and animals move in search of food. Even plants move as they grow and turn toward the sunlight. All this movement is a form of energy, and for thousands of years people have harnessed it for their own use.

FROM PLOWS TO ELECTRICITY

In the past, farmers used the strength of oxen to pull their plows and the energy of running water to turn mills for grinding grain. Now, our energy needs are more complex. We rely on cars, computers, and other advanced machines. Many are powered by electricity, so generating electricity for homes and businesses to use is a huge industry.

Until fairly recently, nearly all of our electricity was generated by burning natural fuels such as coal, oil, or natural gas. But burning these fuels harms the environment, and one day they will run out altogether. Scientists are working on other ways to meet our energy needs by harnessing the motion of the natural world. One of the most promising methods is by using wind to generate electricity.

IN THE NETHERLANDS, WINDMILLS PUMP EXCESS WATER FROM THE GROUND TO HELP FARMERS GROW CROPS.

5

Wind is simply the movement of incredibly tiny molecules that make up the air. They are constantly moving around, bumping into each other and other objects, then bouncing back to collide with something else. The force that these moving molecules exert is called air pressure.

Air pressure is higher in some places and lower in others. As a general rule, the more air molecules there are in an area, the higher the air pressure will be. When sunshine warms an area of air over land, the air expands and rises higher into the sky. This leaves an area of low pressure beneath. Cooler air from an area of high pressure will move to fill the space left by the rising warm air. This movement creates wind.

HERON'S ORGAN

An engineer named Heron of Alexandria lived in Egypt about 2,000 years ago. He used the energy of wind to power a machine. Heron invented a pipe organ attached to a windmill. When the wind blew, it raised and lowered a piston, forcing air through the organ pipes to make sounds.

High pressure

Low pressure

High pressure

Low pressure

THE WINDS THAT BLOW AROUND THE
EARTH MOVE FROM AREAS OF HIGH
PRESSURE TO LOW PRESSURE.

HOW DOES IT WORK?

People were using the wind's energy long before Heron of Alexandria's machine. In ancient Egypt, the wind pushed sailboats up and down the Nile River. Even today—5,000 years later—sailboats are still a common sight.

Just as wind can fill the sail on a boat and push it along, it can also fill the sails of a windmill and make it turn. The first windmills were built more than 1,000 years ago. They captured the energy of the wind and used it to turn a heavy millstone, grinding grain into flour. The idea slowly spread across Asia and into Europe, and by the 12th century windmills were a fairly common sight.

WINDMILLS FOR FARMING

Before long, windmills had been adapted to another use: pumping water. In the Netherlands, these windmills drained land to make it suitable for farming. In other places, the windmills drew water from deep underground so that it could be used for watering crops or animals. In the late 19th century, small water-pumping windmills were built on farms across the United States. Instead of a few large sails, like old-fashioned windmills, these had many smaller steel blades.

FELUCCAS OF THE NILE

The first sailboats on the Nile River were made of reeds. Wooden sailboats called feluccas replaced them to transport goods and people.

FELUCCAS ARE POWERED BY WIND BLOWING INTO THEIR SAILS. SAILORS CAN USE OARS IF THERE IS NO WIND.

ELECTRIC MOTORS

The first electric motors were built in the early 19th century, but they were little more than a curiosity. Electricity was not widely used to power machines until decades later. Cities began to be lit by electric lights in the 1870s, and homes were not far behind. Engineers needed to find reliable ways of generating electricity to power these lights, and wind was one of the options.

An American engineer named Charles Brush built a wind turbine in 1888 that charged batteries stored in the basement of his house in Cleveland, Ohio. It was the first house in the city to be powered by electricity. Over the next few decades, engineers worked on improving the design of wind turbines to make them more efficient.

BLYTH'S MILL

The Scottish engineer James Blyth built a windmill with cloth sails in the garden of his cottage in 1887. It produced enough electricity to power the lights in his home.

NOT VERY EFFICIENT

Charles Brush's windmill was huge but didn't produce much energy. It had 144 blades but could only power 100 light bulbs.

11

INSIDE A TURBINE

Inside a wind turbine, the blades turn an axle connected to the gearbox. The gears accelerate the rotation of the blades. The fast-spinning shaft then spins inside the generator, producing electricity.

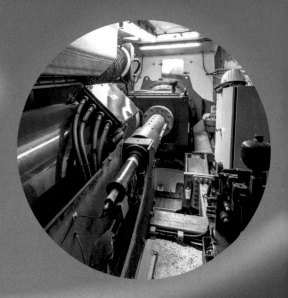

Starting in the 1970s, people looked at ways to use wind power to generate electricity on a much larger scale. They refined the basic design of wind turbines, making them bigger, cheaper to produce, and more efficient.

A modern wind turbine has three main parts: the turbine itself (made of two or three spinning blades), a gearbox, and a generator. These three parts are mounted at the top of a tall tower. The blades are curved and angled to catch the wind, which makes the turbine rotate slowly as the wind blows.

Modern wind turbines on land can be 330 feet (100 m) tall, and some of the ones installed at sea are even taller. The blades are often 115 feet (35 m) long. These enormous windmills can generate a lot of electricity, which is sent through wires to wherever it is needed.

RECORD BREAKER

The Smith–Putnam wind turbine started generating electricity in 1941. It was the biggest wind turbine ever built until 1979.

THE SMITH-PUTNAM WIND TURBINE
AT GRANDPA'S KNOB, VERMONT.

In the past, it was common for wind turbines to be installed by themselves. For example, a farm might have a single turbine to provide electricity. Today, energy companies often install dozens of wind turbines in a single area. This is called a wind farm, and a large one can provide electricity for tens of thousands of homes.

Not all locations are ideal for harnessing wind power, so it makes sense to group turbines together in the best locations. The ideal site has a fairly constant flow of wind of at least 10 miles per hour (16 km/h), with little risk of very high winds that might damage the turbines. Some of the best locations are in high, flat areas such as open plains or rounded hilltops. Many are near the coast, where winds blow in off the sea.

HUGE TRUCKS ARE NEEDED TO TRANSPORT TURBINE BLADES TO INSTALLATION SITES.

CARBON FIBER BLADES

Many turbine blades are made of glass fiber, but new designs often use carbon fiber instead. It is more expensive than glass fiber, but it is lighter and stronger, so blades can be made longer without adding extra weight. Longer blades can generate more electricity.

Winds are often stronger and faster out at sea, so wind turbines placed there can produce even more electricity. Many of these offshore wind farms are being built in northern Europe, as well as in the United States and China. The largest offshore wind farms are made up of more than 100 turbines working together.

Many offshore wind farms are built where the sea is still fairly shallow, with turbines that are fixed to the seabed. Wind farms in deeper areas can use floating turbines. The term "offshore" can also include wind turbines in lakes, fjords, and other inland waters.

Most offshore wind farms are built in waters less than 100 feet (30 m) deep. Engineers drive a large steel tube deep into the seabed up to 100 feet (30 m), then erect the turbine on top of that. In slightly deeper waters, bigger bases are needed to support the turbines. Offshore turbines often have much bigger blades than onshore turbines. However, the part of the tower that sticks up above the water doesn't need to be as tall, because the winds are more constant at low heights than they would be over land.

THE BIGGEST

Work has started to build the world's biggest offshore wind farm. The Hornsea farm is in the North Sea, off the east coast of England, and will produce the electricity to power one million homes.

16

CONSTRUCTION

The gearbox and generator of a modern wind turbine are placed in the nacelle (right), which sits atop a steel tower. Once the nacelle is in place, the rotary blades can be attached to it.

AN OFFSHORE WIND FARM WITH MANY TURBINES.

GOOD AND BAD

There are a lot of reasons why governments would like to use more wind power. It is a type of energy known as "renewable." This means that the source of the energy—in this case, the wind—will never be used up or run out. As long as the Sun heats up the Earth's air, there will be wind.

Other types of fuels, such as oil, coal, and natural gas, are not renewable. These "fossil fuels" were formed deep underground from the remains of plants and animals, a process that took millions of years. Once we have extracted all the oil that exists, there will be no more. This is why renewable sources of energy are so important.

AIR POLLUTION

Fossil fuels have other problems, too. When we burn them to release energy, they release gases that pollute the air. Air pollution can harm plants and animals. Fossil fuels also release carbon dioxide when they are burned. When too much carbon dioxide collects in the Earth's atmosphere, it can cause a rise in global temperature. Once they are up and running, wind turbines don't produce pollution, carbon dioxide, or other harmful emissions, so their energy is cleaner.

WHEN COAL AND OTHER FOSSIL FUELS
ARE BURNED TO GENERATE ELECTRICITY,
SMOKE IS RELEASED INTO THE AIR.

19

Wind power is more than just renewable and clean—it is also very flexible. Wind turbines can be installed in a variety of locations, both onshore and offshore. They can range from a single small turbine providing electricity for a house, to a large turbine powering 600 or more homes.

EXTRA INCOME

Wind turbines do not take up much space. They can't be placed too close together, but the land between them can be used for other things, such as growing crops. Farmers can add to their income by installing wind turbines in their fields and selling the electricity to the national grid.

Installing wind turbines can be expensive, but once the turbines are up and running, they are very cheap to keep going. Wind is free, and modern turbines cost very little to maintain.

DUAL PURPOSE

A french company has built a wind turbine that produces water from humid air as well as generating electricity. The turbine condenses water from the air and then purifies it for drinking.

VERTICAL AXIS

Not all wind turbines have the same design. Vertical axis turbines have their gearbox and generator close to the ground. The Éole wind turbine, at Cap-Chat in Canada, is the largest of this kind.

21

Although wind power has huge potential, it is not without its problems, and one is cost. It can be very expensive to build a wind farm, especially in an offshore location. This means that the energy the wind farm produces may be more expensive than that from a power station burning fossil fuels. Some governments offer subsidies to build turbines. This encourages companies to invest in renewable energy.

UNPREDICTABLE

Wind power is unpredictable because a turbine can only generate electricity when the wind is blowing. So far there is no cost-effective way to store wind energy. The electricity grid needs a consistent source of power, so on a calm day other sources of energy must be used.

Not every location is suitable for wind power. Coasts and hilly areas are often ideal, but not every region has good sites for wind farms. Some countries with promising sites may not be able to afford to invest in wind power.

Wind turbines can be damaged in strong winds. Many turbines shut down automatically when winds reach a certain speed. They do this by changing the angle of the blades, so that they no longer catch the wind and rotate.

Some people find modern wind turbines beautiful, but others don't like the look of them. Wind turbines are often built in the countryside, where they can spoil the view of the natural landscape. They also make noise as they rotate, which can be between 50 and 60 decibels. This is only as loud as an air conditioner, or a conversation at normal volumes. Even so, many people don't want a wind farm built near their home.

Wind turbines can also pose a threat to wildlife. Installing wind farms can damage habitats. And birds, bats, and other flying creatures can be killed if they are hit by a rotating blade.

FAR OUT

Some people do not like the appearance of wind farms. One way of solving this problem is to place them far out at sea, where they can't be seen. In Norway, engineers have tested a type of floating turbine that can be installed in waters up to 2,000 feet (610 m) deep.

TURNING BLADES CAN KILL FLYING
BIRDS, ESPECIALLY WHERE LARGE
FLOCKS GATHER.

THE FUTURE

Wind power is one of the fastest-growing sources of energy. Currently, only about 3 percent of the world's electricity is produced by wind power, but more wind farms are being built every year. Scientists think that by 2030, wind-powered energy production will have increased to 17–19 percent.

Some countries have started to rely heavily on wind power, especially in northern Europe. For example, nearly 40 percent of Denmark's electricity was produced by wind in 2014. Around the world, there are about two dozen countries that have already installed enough turbines to produce 1,000 megawatts or more. One megawatt is enough to power several hundred homes. China is by far the biggest overall producer of wind power. Its wind farms have a combined capacity of more than 145,000 megawatts.

LIVE–IN TURBINE
There are plans to build a wind turbine that people can live in! The Dutch "Windwheel" will have a rotating inner ring that powers the rest of the structure—including apartments and a hotel.

THE WIND FARMS OF THE FUTURE
WILL PROBABLY BE BIGGER AND
HAVE MORE POWERFUL TURBINES.

Engineers are working on new designs for turbines that are more efficient and cheaper to produce. A lot of the research focuses on offshore wind technology, developing turbines that can be installed in deeper water. One idea is to install turbines on offshore oil platforms that are no longer being used for drilling.

Some technologies are completely different from what is in use today. Winds are stronger and more consistent at high altitudes, but traditional turbines just can't be built tall enough to capture them. Scientists are testing a helium balloon, or blimp, that lifts a lightweight turbine into the sky. Other ideas are to construct a series of giant kites to capture the wind's energy, or to launch a tethered aircraft fitted with rotors. Whatever the method of harnessing it, wind power is here to stay.

MINI WINDMILLS

Small wind turbines can be seen on the roofs of many apartment buildings and offices. They all make an important contribution to clean, renewable energy.

THIS BLIMP HAS A WIND TURBINE IN THE MIDDLE. IT FLOATS 1,000 FEET (305 M) ABOVE THE GROUND WHERE THE WIND BLOWS MORE STRONGLY.

GLOSSARY

accelerate: To make go faster.

condense: To change from water vapor into water.

decibel: A unit of sound.

emissions: The discharge of gases and particles into the atmosphere.

gear: A device that quickens or slows the speed of rotation of an axle.

generator: A device that turns mechanical energy into electricity.

helium: A light, colorless gas often used to blow up balloons.

humid: Damp or moist.

megawatt (MW): A large unit of electricity. One MW can provide all the electricity for more than several hundred houses.

molecules: The smallest units of a substance that have all the properties of that substance. Air is made up mostly of molecules of nitrogen and oxygen.

pollution: The release of substances that have harmful or toxic effects into the atmosphere, rivers, or ocean.

subsidies: Grants given by governments to help fund projects.

tethered: Tied to the ground.

turbine: A machine with blades attached to a central rotating shaft. Turbines are used to generate electricity.

FURTHER INFORMATION

BOOKS

Challoner, Jack. *Energy* (Eyewitness).
New York: Dorling Kindersley, 2012.

Doeden, Matt. *Finding Out About Wind Energy*
(Searchlight). New York: Lerner, 2014.

Kopp, Megan. *Energy from Wind: Wind Farming*
(Next Generation Energy). New York: Crabtree, 2015.

WEBSITES

Due to the changing nature of Internet links,
PowerKids Press has developed an online list
of websites related to the subject of this book.
This site is updated regularly. Please use this
link to access the list:

www.powerkidslinks.com/tfop/wind

INDEX